$M$ay your dreams
   never disappear with age,
but may they continue
as alive and as beautiful as you
with the knowledge that they
will someday come true.

— Joanne Domenech

# Don't Ever Give Up Your
# Dreams

## A Blue Mountain Arts® Collection

**Blue Mountain Press**™

SPS Studios, Inc., Boulder, Colorado

We wish to thank Susan Polis Schutz for permission to reprint the following poems that appear in this publication: "This life is yours..." and "If you know...." Copyright © 1978 by Continental Publications. And for "Love Your Life," "You Deserve the Best," and "Find happiness in nature...." Copyright © 1982, 1983 by Stephen Schutz and Susan Polis Schutz. All rights reserved.

We wish to thank Donna Fargo for permission to reprint the poems "I Know You Can Make Your Dreams Come True" and "Reach for the Stars, Go for Your Dreams!" in this publication. Copyright © 2001 by PrimaDonna Entertainment Corp. All rights reserved.

Library of Congress Catalog Card Number: 2001001901
ISBN: 0-88396-637-9 (hardcover) — ISBN: 0-88396-183-0 (trade paper)

ACKNOWLEDGMENTS appear on page 64.

Certain trademarks are used under license.

Manufactured in China
First Printing in Hardcover: June 2002

 This book is printed on recycled paper.

This book is printed on fine quality, laid embossed, 80 lb. paper. This paper has been specially produced to be acid free (neutral pH) and contains no groundwood or unbleached pulp. It conforms with all the requirements of the American National Standards Institute, Inc., so as to ensure that this book will last and be enjoyed by future generations.

### Library of Congress Cataloging-in-Publication Data

Don't ever give up your dreams : a Blue Mountain Arts collection.
        p. cm.
    ISBN 0-88396-637-9 (alk. paper)
    ISBN 0-88396-183-0 (pbk : alk. paper)
    1. Self-actualization (Psychology)—Poetry. 2. American poetry—20$^{th}$ century.
    3. Success—Poetry. I. Blue Mountain Arts (Firm)
    PS595.S45 D66 2001
    811'.5080353—dc21

                                                        2001001901
                                                        CIP

# SPS Studios, Inc.

P.O. Box 4549, Boulder, Colorado 80306

# Contents

# Don't Ever Let Anything
# Stand in the Way of Your Dreams

*Catch the star that holds your destiny —*
*the one that forever twinkles within your heart*
*Take advantage of precious opportunities*
*while they still sparkle before you*
*Always believe that your ultimate goal*
*is attainable as long as*
*you commit yourself to it*
*Though barriers may sometimes*
*stand in the way of your dreams*
*remember that your destiny is hiding behind them*
*Accept the fact that not everyone*
*is going to approve of the choices you make*
*Have faith in your judgment*
*Catch the star that twinkles in your heart*
*and it will lead you to your destiny's path*
*Follow that pathway and uncover the*
*sweet sunrises that await you*
*Take pride in your accomplishments*
*as they are steppingstones to your dreams*
*Understand that you may make mistakes*
*but don't let them discourage you*
*Value your capabilities and talents*
*for they are what make you truly unique*
*You are capable of making*
*your brightest dreams come true*
*Give your hopes everything you've got*
*and you will catch the star that holds your destiny*

*— Shannon M. Lester*

# I Know You Can Make
# Your Dreams Come True

*I am confident that you can do anything you set your mind to. Whatever hopes you have for your future, I believe you can find a way to make your dreams come true.*

*Whatever challenges you face in life, I believe you'll turn every experience into something positive. When you have serious questions you need to answer or emotions you need to process, I know that you'll take your time and do the right thing.*

*Even though there may be times when you'll be dissatisfied with the way things are going in your life, I know you'll learn the lessons you need to learn and eventually make the changes you need to make and move on.*

*I want you to know that I am always thinking of you, praying for you, and wishing you the best. If you need me to talk to about your concerns, I'm here to support you, just like I know you are for me if I need you.*

*You are a bright, sweet, thoughtful, and wonderful human being, and I'll always believe in you.*

*— Donna Fargo*

# Don't Give Up

*I know you're going*
   *to make it...*
*It may take time*
   *and hard work*
*You may become frustrated*
*and at times you'll feel*
   *like giving up*
*Sometimes you may even*
      *wonder if it's really*
         *worth it*
*But I have confidence in you,*
*and I know you'll make it*
   *if you try.*

*— amanda pierce*

You have powers you never dreamed of. You can do things you never thought you could do. There are no limitations in what you can do except the limitations in your own mind as to what you cannot do.

Don't think you cannot.

Think you can.

— Darwin P. Kingsley

You never know
until you try.
And you never try
  unless you _really_ try.
You give it your best shot;
you do the best you can.

And if you've done everything
  in your power, and still "fail" —
the truth of the matter is
  that you haven't failed at all.

When you reach for your dreams,
  no matter what they may be,
  you grow from the reaching;
    you learn from the trying;
      you win from the doing.

— Laine Parsons

*Learning isn't easy...*
*frustration tends to set in quickly.*
*You hurt.*
*You feel defeated.*
*You want to give up —*
    *to quit.*
*You want to walk away*
    *and pretend it doesn't matter.*
*But you won't,*
*because you're not a loser —*
    *you're a fighter...*

*We all have to lose sometimes*
    *before we can win.*
*We have to cry sometimes*
    *before we can smile.*
*We have to hurt*
    *before we can be strong.*
*But if you keep on working*
    *and believing,*
*you'll have victory*
    *in the end.*

*— Ann Davies*

*I am just beginning*
*to make some definite changes*
  *in my life.*
*Some of them will take time,*
*some will cause me grief,*
*some will mean risk*
*and a lot of growing pains, too.*
*But whatever the case,*
*I know I will make it...*

*It's having someone like you*
*to see me through*
*both the good times*
*and the bad*
*that makes me so sure.*

— Gail Nishimoto

*The only way to find rainbows*
*is to look within your heart;*
*the only way to live fairy tales*
*is through the imagination*
*   and power of your mind;*
*the only place to begin*
*   a search for peace*
*is within your very soul;*
*because rainbows,*
*   fairy tales, and peace*
*are treasures that grow*
*from the inside out.*

*— Evelyn K. Tharp*

*This life is yours*
*Take the power*
*to choose what you want to do*
*and do it well*
*Take the power*
*to love what you want in life*
*and love it honestly*
*Take the power*
*to walk in the forest*
*and be a part of nature*
*Take the power*
*to control your own life*
*No one else can do it for you*
*Take the power*
*to make your life*
*healthy*
*exciting*
*worthwhile*
*and very happy*

*— Susan Polis Schutz*

*If* you have a dream
   alive in your mind,
Bring it to the world, give it life.
Too often, the treasures that are
   ours alone to give
are never given the chance to grow.
We each have a unique gift
   to bring to this world.
It is our purpose in life
   to offer this gift.
For even if only a few people
   benefit from our offering,
the world is then a better place
   to live.

                        — Susan Staszewski

# My Prayer...

That I will have the strength
   to carry on,
the patience to try again
   when things go wrong,
the ability to see beauty
   where others see none.
That I will have the hope
   of a new dream
      waiting to be dreamed,
the chance to reach out,
and the wisdom to look forward
to tomorrow.

              — Donna Wayland

*Hold fast your dreams!*
*Within your heart*
*Keep one still, secret spot*
*Where dreams may go,*
*And, sheltered so,*
*May thrive and grow*
*Where doubt and fear are not.*
*O keep a place apart,*
*Within your heart,*
*For little dreams to go!*

*We see so many ugly things —*
*Deceits and wrongs and quarrelings:*
*We know, alas! we know*
*How quickly fade*
*The color in the west,*
*The bloom upon the flower.*
*The bloom upon the breast*
*And youth's blind hour.*
*Yet keep within your heart*
*A place apart*
*Where little dreams may go,*
*May thrive and grow.*
*Hold fast — hold fast your dreams!*

— Louise Driscoll

# Love Your Life

We cannot
listen to what
others want us
to do
We must listen
to ourselves
Society
family
friends
mates
do not know what
we must do
Only we know
and only we
can do what is
right for us
So start
right now
You will need to
work very hard

*You will need to*
*overcome many obstacles*
*You will need to go*
*against the better*
*judgment of many people*
*and you will need to*
*bypass their prejudices*
*But you can have*
*whatever you want*
*if you*
*try hard*
*enough*
*So start right now and*
*you will live*
*a life designed*
*by you and*
*for you*
*and you will*
*love*
*your*
*life*

*— Susan Polis Schutz*

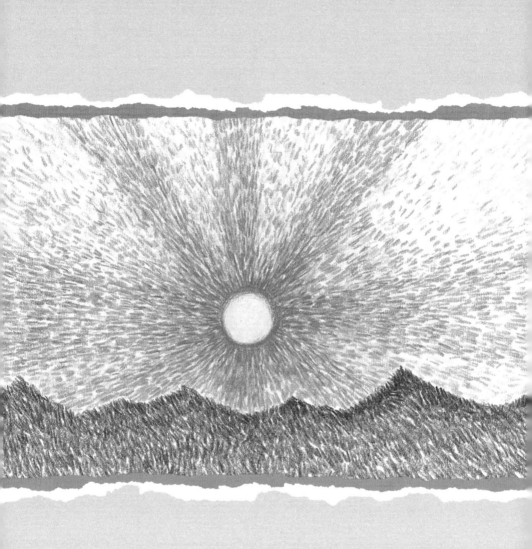

*Life is a series of*
*beginnings...*
*that bring us closer*
*to the realization of*
*our dreams.*

*May all your*
*beginnings*
*be showered by sunbeams*
*and all your dreams*
*sense the warmth*
*of success.*

— Edith Schaffer Lederberg

*A dreamer lives for eternity.*

— *Anonymous*

# For a Happy Life...

Believe in yourself
    but don't be overconfident;
Be satisfied
    but know that you can always improve;
Accept love graciously
    and always be ready to give more;
Be modest in victory and success
    and courageous in defeat;
Give comfort and security to others
    and you will always receive it in return;
Be glad... just for being
    the wonderful person that you are.

— Lee Wilkinson

*Set yourself earnestly*
*to see what you are made to do,*
*and then set yourself earnestly*
*to do it...*
*and the loftier your purpose is,*
*the more sure you will be*
*to make the world richer*
*with every enrichment*
*of yourself.*

— *Phillips Brooks*

*Deep within our hearts,*
*each of us carries the seed*
*of a secret dream,*
*special and unique to each individual.*
*Sometimes another person*
*can share that dream*
*and help it grow to fulfillment;*
*other times, the dream remains*
*a solitary pursuit, known only*
*to the seeker. But secret or shared,*
*no matter what it might be,*
*a dream is a potential which*
*should never be discouraged. For*
*each of us also carries within ourselves*
*a light which can cause the seed*
*to grow and blossom into beautiful reality...*
*that same light I've seen shine*
*so clearly in you.*

*— Edmund O'Neill*

*The courage of working for
something you believe in,
day in and day out,
    year after year,
can be difficult
    but holds the greatest rewards.*

*Find your ideal...
    and follow it.*

— V. Sukomlin

## Be All that You Can Be

*Champion the right to be yourself.
Dare to be different
    and to set your own pattern;
Live your own life,
    and follow your own star.*

— Lin Yutang

# If You Think You Can, You Can

Your mind is your real self —
   your real being.
There are more and more possibilities in nature,
in the elements, in man and out of man;
and they come as fast as man sees
and knows how to use these forces,
in nature and in himself.

Possibilities and miracles
   mean the same thing.

— Prentice Mulford

*We grow great by dreams.*
*Dreamers… see things*
   *in the soft haze of a spring day,*
*or in the red fire*
*of a long winter's evening.*
*Some of us let these great dreams die,*
*but others nourish and protect them,*
*nurse them through bad days*
*till they bring them to*
*the sunshine and light*
*which comes always to those*
*who sincerely hope that*
*their dreams*
*will come true.*

*— Woodrow Wilson*

*Today,* we share
words and beginnings,
hopes and songs,
expectations for the future —
built from yesterday,
built from now.

*Tomorrow...*
watercolors and rainbows,
impressions and soft scenes,
a tapestry of feelings —
weaved from memories,
weaved from dreams.

— Albert M. Ward

*Just as no one can
    tell you how to feel
about a beautiful sunset,
no one can tell you how
    to live your life.
You are the artist...
and must shape your
    experiences
with your own hand.*

— Susan Staszewski

$W$e can do
anything we want to
if we stick to it
long enough.

— Helen Keller


$F$ollow your dreams
and pursue them with courage
for it is the pursuit
of those dreams
that makes life
really worth living.

— Linda DuPuy Moore

*I* dream of beauty
  that transcends time
in a world that knows
  nothing else
Where all is clean and pure
  and good
and all mankind is willing
  to help one another
Where discovery is a way of life
and there is no fear of failure
Where God is a very personal
  thing that is real to everyone
I dream of a time that has
  no pain
and where there is no despair
Where love has a constant meaning
that keeps people together forever
I dream that all this could
  someday be true
and I pray that I will share
  it all
    with you

— Johnnie Rosenauer

*Let* every day
be a dream
we can touch.

Let every day
be a love
we can feel.

Let every day
be a reason
to live.

— Claudia Adrienne Grandi

*I* believe that we cannot live better
than in seeking to become
still better than we are.

— Socrates

*D*on't waste precious time
worrying about
what you should have done...
But rather, focus your attention
on what you are doing now,
and what you want to do
in the future
Don't concentrate
on any mistakes that might
    have been made,
but learn from them.

— Debbie Avery

$A$ *thing*
*that you*
*sincerely*
*believe in*
*cannot*
*be wrong.*

— D. H. Lawrence

$T$*he best of life*
*is that which*
*ever reaches upward*
*and strives toward*
*better things.*

— James R. Miller

*If* it should happen
*that your dreams*
*are shattered,*
*do not be afraid.*
*Have the courage*
*to pick up the pieces*
*and smile at the world.*
*For dreams that are*
*easily shattered*
*can just as easily*
*be rebuilt.*

— *Chris Jensen*

*F*ind happiness in nature
in the beauty of a mountain
in the serenity of the sea
Find happiness in friendship
in the fun of doing things together
in the sharing and understanding
Find happiness in your family
in the stability of knowing
    that someone cares
in the strength of love and honesty
Find happiness in yourself
in your mind and body
in your values and achievements
Find happiness in
everything
you
do

— Susan Polis Schutz

*I like you...*
*You feel life way down inside.*
*You have the courage to think*
*and the strength to get*
*     involved.*
*You are a dreamer...*
*and dreamers are too rare...*
*For few people believe*
*     enough to dream.*

*— Linda S. Smith*

*I wish for you to
be happy,
and to reach
    for the best...
for what is happiness,
if not to believe in
and follow
one's dream?*

— *Theophile Gautier*

*It's natural to feel disappointed*
   *when things don't go your way*
*It's easy to think...*
   *"I can't do it, so why try?"*
*But no matter how scared you are*
   *of making a mistake*
*or how discouraged you may become,*
*never give up...*
*because if you don't try and*
*if you don't go after what you*
   *want in life,*
*it won't come to you,*
*and you'll be forced to accept*
   *things that you know could*
      *be better...*

*Success is not measured by*
   *whether you win or*
      *whether you fail —*
*there's always a little bit*
   *of success, even if things*
      *don't go your way —*
*What's important is that you'll*
   *feel better about yourself,*
      *for the simple reason*
         *that you tried.*

— *amanda pierce*

*If you know*
*who you are and*
*what you want and*
*why you want it*
*and if you have*
*confidence in yourself and*
*a strong will to obtain your desires and*
*a very positive attitude*
*you can make*
*your life*
*yours*
*if you ask*

*— Susan Polis Schutz*

$O$ne day at a time —
this is enough.
Do not look back
and grieve over the past,
for it is gone;
and do not be troubled
about the future,
for it has not yet come.
Live in the present,
and make it so beautiful
that it will be worth
remembering.

— Ida Scott Taylor

*There is a funny old saying that says,*
*"If you don't ride a bicycle,*
*you don't fall off!"*
*What it means to say, of course, is that*
*if you do put a lot of energy into something,*
*you are bound to make mistakes;*
*and if you take a lot of risks,*
*you are bound to tumble here and there.*
*But remember this: if you persist,*
*you will arrive at the destination of your choice.*
*And if you do occasionally fall in the process,*
*you'll learn much more than if you don't.*

*So try, and do, and discover all that you can be.*

*And take me with you...*
*    in spirit, as you go,*
*so you'll know that*
*I'll always be beside you*
*wishing for nothing but the best.*

*— Michael Rille*

*In*
*your moment of success —*
*I wish for you*
*a greater mountain to climb,*
*a wider sea to sail,*
*a more profound challenge to meet —*
*for it has been*
*the journey to the summit,*
*the reaching for distant shores,*
*the tenacity to answer the call*
*    that has made you*
*    the most special person you are today.*

*— Kele Daniels*

$D$on't ever give up your dreams...
and never leave them behind.
Find them; make them yours,
and all through your life,
cherish them,
  and never let them go.

— Elisa Costanza

# You Deserve the Best

A person will get only what he or she wants
You must choose your goals carefully
Know what you like
and what you do not like
Be critical about what you can do well
and what you cannot do well
Choose a career or lifestyle that interests you
and work hard to make it a success
Enter a relationship that is worthy of everything
you are physically and mentally
Be honest with people, help them if you can
but don't depend on anyone to make life easy
or happy for you
Only you can do that for yourself
Strive to achieve all that you like
Find happiness in everything you do
Love with your entire being
Make a triumph
of every aspect
of your life

— Susan Polis Schutz

# Reach for the Stars,
# Go for Your Dreams!

*There are rainbows and pots of gold waiting
for you over the horizon, surprises and gifts
and wonders just around every corner. Look
forward to them. Love them. Catch these
pieces of life as they come, and hold them
close to you. Savor every moment, every
triumph, and even every failure. Don't be
afraid to be too passionate to enjoy the ride,
chase every quest, and praise every hint of
answers to your questions. Dream big. Work
hard. Enjoy your play time. Deal with all the
challenges in life like the true champ you are.
You may not always get what you want, but
you're never a failure if you give it your all
and do the best you can.*

*You don't have to be perfect or the smartest person in the world to dream. You don't have to have all the answers or know everything to make your dream come true. Dreams are free, but they belong to the dreamer who'll take a chance.*

*So let your imagination take you to that perfect place where there is nothing to be afraid of and you can have anything you want. Prepare yourself. Knock on the door of opportunity, and be ready when it answers. Celebrate all the possibilities. Your future is full of hope and happy times, fantasies, and lessons to learn. Learn them well. Enjoy each one. Be good. Believe in miracles. Believe that all things are possible. Love and allow yourself to be loved. Reach for the stars and go for your dreams.*

— *Donna Fargo*

# "Words of Wisdom"

## *That Will Keep a Smile on Your Face,*
## *Keep Your Motivation in Place,*
## *and Help Your Dreams Come True*

You're good, but you're going to be great ❧ You're the
best, but you're going to get better ❧ Sometimes the paths
we take are long and hard, but remember: those are
always the ones that lead to the most beautiful views ❧
Challenges come along, inevitably; how you respond to
them determines who you are — deep down inside —
and everything you're going to be ❧ Increase the chances
of reaching your goals by working at them gradually ❧
The very best you can do is all that is asked of you ❧
Realize that you are capable of working miracles of your
own making ❧ Remember that opportunities have a reason
for knocking on your door, and the right ones are there
for the taking ❧ You don't always have to win, but you
do need to know what it takes to be a winner ❧ It's up
to you to find the key that unlocks the door to a more
fulfilling life ❧ Understand that increased difficulty brings
you nearer to the truth of how to survive it — and get
beyond it ❧ Cross your bridges ❧ Meet your challenges ❧
Reach out for your dreams, and bring them closer and
closer to your heart ❧ Get rid of the "if only's," and get
on with whatever you need to do to get things right ❧
Go after what you want in life, with all the blessings of
all the people who care about you ❧ And find out what
making your wishes come true really feels like ❧

— Collin McCarty

# ACKNOWLEDGMENTS

*The following is a partial list of authors whom the publisher especially wishes to thank for permission to reprint their works.*

*Joanne Domenech for "May your dreams...." Copyright © 1981 by Joanne Domenech. Shannon M. Lester for "Don't Ever Let Anything Stand in the Way of Your Dreams." Copyright © 2001 by Shannon M. Lester. Evelyn K. Tharp for "The only way...." Copyright © 1983 by Evelyn K. Tharp. Susan Staszewski for "If you have a dream..." and "Just as no one can...." Copyright © 1983 by Susan Staszewski. Donna Wayland for "My Prayer...." Copyright © 1983 by Donna Wayland. Edith Schaffer Lederberg for "Life is a series...." Copyright © 1983 by Edith Schaffer Lederberg. Lee Wilkinson for "For a Happy Life...." Copyright © 1983 by Lee Wilkinson. Albert M. Ward for "Today, we share words...." Copyright © 1983 by Albert M. Ward. Linda DuPuy Moore for "Follow your dreams...." Copyright © 1983 by Linda DuPuy Moore. Johnnie Rosenauer for "I dream of beauty...." Copyright © 1983 by Johnnie Rosenauer. Claudia Adrienne Grandi for "Let every day...." Copyright © 1983 by Claudia Adrienne Grandi. Debbie Avery for "Don't waste precious time...." Copyright © 1983 by Debbie Avery. Chris Jensen for "If it should happen...." Copyright © 1983 by Chris Jensen. Linda S. Smith for "I like you...." Copyright © 1983 by Linda S. Smith. Kele Daniels for "In your moment of...." Copyright © 1983 by Kele Daniels. All rights reserved.*

*The following works have previously appeared in Blue Mountain Arts® publications:*

*"Learning isn't easy..." by Ann Davies. Copyright © 1983 by Ann Davies. "I am just beginning..." by Gail Nishimoto. Copyright © 1983 by Gail Nishimoto. "Don't ever give up..." by Elisa Costanza. Copyright © 1981 by Elisa Constanza. All rights reserved.*

*"Don't Give Up" and "It's natural to feel..." by amanda pierce, "You never know until..." by Laine Parsons, "Deep within our hearts..." by Edmund O'Neill, "There is a funny old saying..." by Michael Rille, and "'Words of Wisdom'" by Collin McCarty. Copyright © 1983 by SPS Studios, Inc. All rights reserved.*

*A careful effort has been made to trace the ownership of poems used in this anthology in order to obtain permission to reprint copyrighted materials and give proper credit to the copyright owners. If any error or omission has occurred, it is completely inadvertent, and we would like to make corrections in future editions provided that written notification is made to the publisher:*

*SPS STUDIOS, INC., P.O. Box 4549, Boulder, Colorado 80306.*